EFENCE OF THE REALM is the fascinating story going back over 2,000 years across the central area of Southern England encompassing Hampshire, the Solent, and the Isle of Wight.

For 2,000 years or more this remarkable area has seen armies come and go as it has played a key part in the defence of this country. In this area of rolling downland and sheltered waters you will discover Portsmouth, the traditional home of the Royal Navy; Aldershot, the first permanent home of the British Army; Farnborough, the birthplace of British aviation; and Gosport, the home of the Submarine Service. There is also the historic city of Winchester and the commercial port of Southampton.

The Defence of the Realm area has been endowed with a unique collection of castles, museums, great ships and stately homes. As military and naval requirements have changed, so many of these sites have been opened to the public giving local residents and visitors the opportunity to discover more of this fascinating story.

This book provides an introduction to the Defence of the Realm story which, hopefully, will encourage you to visit some of the sites themselves.

Edited by Nicola Horsey, General Manager, Defence of the Realm. Contributions and assistance from Graham Bishop, Stephen Brooks, Richard Compton-Hall, Councillor Emery-Wallis, Malcolm George, Nicholas Hall, Mike Hughes, John Reed, Jo Thorpe and Colin White.

# CONTENTS

Design: Haven Design Group and R. Wilcockson

First published 1992

ISBN 0 7110 2086 8

Published by Ian Allan Ltd, Shepperton, Surrey; and printed by Ian Allan Printing Ltd at their works at Coombelands in Runnymede, England.

# THE DECLINE
# OF THE ROMAN EMPIRE

HE SOUTH COAST of England had been an important trading route for many centuries. In particular the sheltered waters of the Solent — its river estuaries and natural harbours — were an added attraction.

It was at Hengistbury Head, at the head of Christchurch harbour, and in the Chichester harbour area that two of these early trading places were established in the centuries before the Roman Conquest in AD 43.

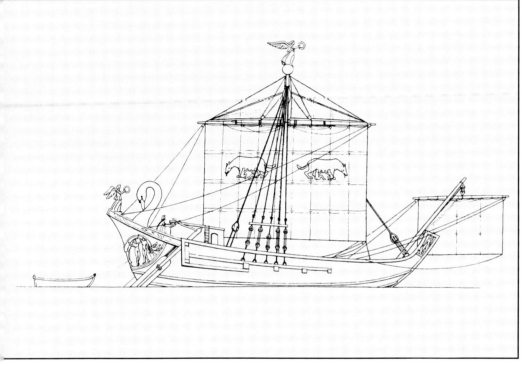

**A Roman ship from 200AD.**

Aerial view of Portchester Castle.

The Roman walls, Portchester Castle, *English Heritage*

The romanisation of Hampshire and the Isle of Wight quickly took place. The late Iron Age tribal centres of Silchester, Chichester and Winchester became important towns under Roman administration, connected by a network of newly-built roads. All three towns were provided with stone walls by the 3rd century AD.

Bitterne, on the outskirts of Southampton, became a trading port. It was probably established in the early years of Roman rule and appears by the late 4th century to have acquired stone-built defences.

As well as the palace complex at Fishbourne, a number of Roman villas were also established along the coast between Portsmouth and Chichester in the 2nd century AD. In recent years excavations at Hayling Island have revealed an important pagan temple, the largest ever found in Roman Britain.

By the middle of the 3rd century the Roman Empire was facing external threats from Germanic tribes in eastern Europe. As one of the consequences town walls were strengthened and a string of forts were built to defend both sides of the Channel.

The fort at Portchester was built sometime after 286AD by Carausius, possibly as a fleet base for clearing the Channel of Saxon pirates. Carausius had been in command of the Channel fleet before setting himself up as a rival to the legitimate Emperor. He was, however, deposed by 293AD.

Portchester continued in intermittent use until the late 4th century by which time the end of Roman Britain was in sight. Many of the regional towns, like Silchester, were already in decline. Sometime in the early 5th century the Roman administration began to collapse and Roman troops withdrawn to assist in the defence of the Empire in Gaul. For England the Dark Ages had begun.

**A coin bearing a portrait of Carausius.** *Portsmouth City Museums*

**Roman Hampshire.**

**1 PORTCHESTER CASTLE**
A Roman fort, a Norman castle and church share the same attractive site on the north shore of Portsmouth Harbour. An exhibition in the Keep presents its long and eventful history.

# INVASIONS
# AND SETTLEMENTS

URING THE 5TH CENTURY Saxon invaders became settlers and indeed some were already serving as mercenaries in the Roman army stationed in Britain. Further migrations of Saxons and Jutes took place over the next hundred years or so and evidence of their settlements and cemeteries has come to light in archaeological excavations along the coastal regions in Hampshire and the Isle of Wight.

An Anglo-Saxon England was growing up to rival Roman Britain in its culture and wealth. The West Saxon kings had established one of the country's earliest cathedrals at Winchester by the late 7th century. The rapid spread of Christianity throughout Wessex was undertaken by a network of minster churches like that surviving at Titchfield, near the coast. By the 10th century the Old Minster at Winchester had become one of the greatest churches in western European Christendom and a pilgrimage centre for the venerated remains of St Swithun.

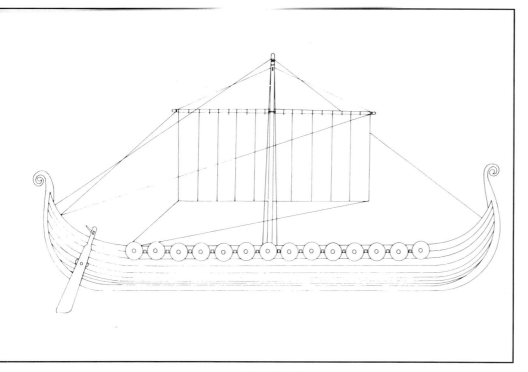

**A Viking longship.**

Also in the 7th century a trading port was established at Hamwic, Saxon Southampton. There mercantile links were forged with other north European ports like Rouen in Normandy. English missionaries like Boniface and Willibald were trained at early monastic centres at Nursling and Bishop's Waltham before departing from the Hampshire coast for the continent.

In the 9th century Viking raids threatened the country including attacks on Winchester and Southampton. In 871 the systematic ravaging of Wessex by the Danes coincided with the accession of Alfred to the English throne.

By the early 10th century Alfred and his son Edward had established a network of fortified towns called 'burhs' across southern England at places like Chichester, Christchurch and Southampton and did much to develop urban life. At Winchester and Portchester the stout Roman walls provided an ideal place in which to establish 'burhs'.

The recorded beginnings of the English navy lie in the small fleet of ships built by Alfred in the hope of defeating the Danes at sea off the coasts of Hampshire and the Isle of Wight.

On the death of Edward the Confessor in 1065, Harold was crowned the last Saxon king of England. However, William, Duke of Normandy, claimed that Edward had promised him the throne and consequently made plans to invade England – which he did in September 1066 and opened up a new chapter in English history.

King Alfred's statue, Winchester.

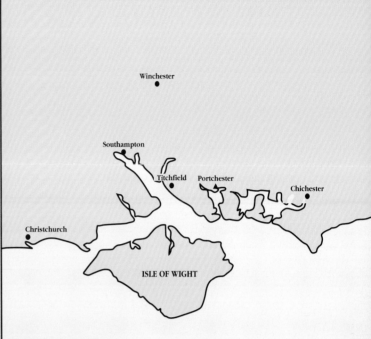

Anglo-Saxon Hampshire.

1    SAXON CHURCH
St Nicholas Church, South
Boarhunt, a Saxon church in
Hampshire.

2    SAXON TOWER
The Saxon west tower of
Titchfield Church in Hampshire.

# THE NORMAN CONQUEST

 S THE NAME suggests, 'Normandy' was a province in north-west France in which a Frankish king invited Norsemen or 'northmen' to settle. It became the base for a series of ambitious leaders to establish one of the most powerful states in medieval Europe with wide trading links and territorial claims. By the start of the 11th century Normandy had strong links with the English crown and Norman influence had been strong at Edward the Confessor's court. In 1035 William became Duke of Normandy and in the 1050s was also recognised as heir to the English throne.

When Harold proclaimed himself King of England, William gathered his forces and in September 1066 sailed across the Channel, landing at Pevensey. The Battle of Hastings was fought on 14 October, William was victorious and marched through Kent and the home counties before taking London where he was crowned the first Norman king of England on Christmas Day.

**The New Forest established by the Normans as a Royal Hunting Forest.**

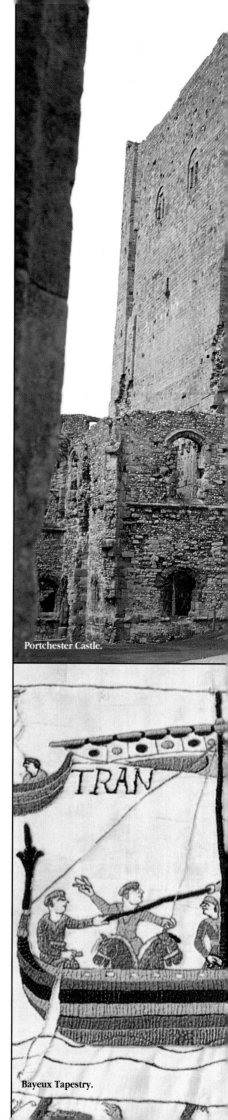

**Portchester Castle.**

**Bayeux Tapestry.**

Within a year William had secured the royal treasury at Winchester and ordered a castle to be built there under the supervision of William Fitz Osbern, his friend and ally. Fitz Osbern was also responsible for the building of the castle at Carisbrooke on the Isle of Wight in the 1070s.

Other strong Norman castles were constructed in the region in the late 11th and first half of the 12th century like Portchester, Southampton, Christchurch and Basing. Portchester remained a royal stronghold and residence benefiting from its convenience as an embarkation point for Normandy.

Hampshire was a particularly favoured area with the Norman kings. Winchester was the joint capital with London until the end of the 12th century, and from here came the Domesday Book in 1086. Southampton flourished as a royal port trading with France and the Low Countries. Norman merchants settled in the town and the remains of some of their houses and cellar warehouses (undercrofts) can still be seen. The nearby New Forest was established as a royal hunting forest during William's reign.

Portsmouth was founded towards the end of the 12th century as was Lymington — both by Norman aristocrats, although Portsmouth's potential was soon realised by the Crown who seized it as a royal possession and granted it a charter in 1194.

Basing ▲

Winchester ●

Southampton ●

Portchester ⚙

Portsmouth ●

Lymington ●

Christchurch ●

Carisbrooke Castle ▲

**ISLE OF WIGHT**

**Norman sites.**

SIVII

**1 MEDIEVAL MERCHANT'S HOUSE**
Restored by English Heritage, this
Norman house is open to the public in
Southampton and dates back to about
1290.

**2 WINCHESTER CATHEDRAL**
This is a model of Winchester
Cathedral as it was in Norman times.
Founded in 1079, it is the largest
medieval cathedral in Europe and one
of the most beautiful. It is where
William II is buried, Henry VII was
baptised and Mary Tudor married
Philip of Spain.

# THE HUNDRED YEARS' WAR

HE HUNDRED YEARS' WAR was not a continuous war, but part of a series of disjointed conflicts between English and French monarchs. Throughout its duration (1337-1453), the coastal towns of Hampshire were to be the centre of much military activity. Ironically this was also to prove a period of prosperity, especially in the 15th century.

Edward III started by sending small expeditionary forces into Northern France, but the action was not all one way. In 1336 a squadron of French warships attacked several of the English fleet anchored off the Isle of Wight. Some ships were scuttled and others boarded and taken off to Normandy to be sold as war prizes. A more severe blow was dealt in 1338 when the French raided Portsmouth and Southampton. However, in 1340 Edward destroyed the French fleet off Sluys which gave England mastery of the Channel for the next 30 years.

In 1346 Edward III collected an army of approximately 20,000 men at Portchester, the best organised force to be seen in Britain since the Roman legions. They landed at St-Vaast-de-la-Hogue, near Cherbourg, and their march through Normandy and Picardy culminated in the overwhelming victory at Crécy on 26 August.

Meanwhile, back in England, Edward had ordered the construction of fortifications for Southampton which were finally finished by the late 14th century. Today the town walls and surviving gates are the finest Hundred Years' War urban defences in England. Portsmouth did not complete its defences until the early 15th century. The Round Tower in

provinces in south-west France.

Henry V came to the throne in 1413 with a greater determination to reassert his French claims. He brought his fleet up to strength by building ships in Southampton and Bursledon. The remains of one of his larger ships the *Grace Dieu* lies in the mudflats of the River Hamble.

In 1415 Henry collected together a large army which was quartered at Southampton and Portchester together with some of the new weapons of war — artillery. He sailed with his forces from the Solent area in August and landed at Harfleur in Normandy. Despite losing a third of his army besieging Harfleur, he still went on to a

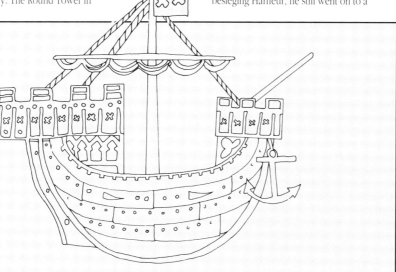

**A medieval ship of around 1325.**

Old Portsmouth dates from this period.

There was a period of peace from 1348 to 1354 at a time when the Black Death was sweeping across both countries. In 1355 Edward III was at Portchester again with troops which, combined with those of his son, the Black Prince, led to the capture of the French king in 1356. The king was later exchanged for a huge ransom and English sovereignty over Aquitaine, Calais and Ponthieu in France.

Other expeditions left from Portchester during the 1360s and there were retaliatory French raids on Portsmouth, Gosport, the Isle of Wight and Lymington. During the later years of the century the French navy was rebuilt which made it difficult for England to supply her

decisive victory over the French at Agincourt.

To show that they were unbowed, the French blockaded Southampton a year later and being unsuccessful in taking the town, ravaged the nearby coast. Henry VI was less than a year old when his father died in 1422, and with France reinvigorated through the efforts of Joan of Arc, a truce was sought.

Henry VI's marriage to Margaret of Anjou, cousin to the French king, in 1445, was agreed in order to secure the peace. The royal wedding, which took place at Titchfield Abbey, was a fitting end to the Hundred Years' War in England. In France activities finally ceased with the defeat of the English army at Castillon, in the Dordogne, in July 1453.

The Round Tower, Old Portsmouth.

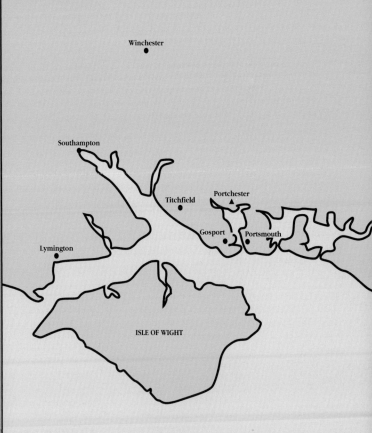

Hampshire during the Hundred Years' War.

**1**                    **WINCHESTER'S WESTGATE**

One of the medieval gateways to Winchester, the Westgate was refortified in the late 14th century against French attacks. It became a debtor's prison in the 17th century and is now a museum. *John Crook*

9

# THE TUDORS

ITH THE DYNASTIC in-fighting known as the 'Wars of the Roses' (1453, 1455-71), the English monarchs were more concerned with internal politics than anything else. There were virtually no English royal naval forces between the 1440s and the advent of the Tudor dynasty in 1485.

Up to this time such troops as were required at home or overseas were raised at the time by the aristocracy as part of their service to the monarch or were recruited by the Lords Lieutenant of the Counties. They were entirely untrained, and the army raised in 1588 to face the expected Spanish invasion was described as a rabble in contemporary accounts. It was during this period that the Militia was formed involving a form of part-time conscripted service, organised on a county basis by the Lords Lieutenant, each county being required to fill a quota determined by the Government. It could be, and periodically was, embodied for long periods.

Henry VII had a small fleet of ships, and to help maintain them, he established the earliest known dry dock at Portsmouth, in 1495. This was the origin of Portsmouth naval base, now the oldest working naval installation in the world.

The fleet was expanded by his son, Henry VIII, who built new, broadside-firing warships to serve in his wars with France. One of these vessels was the *Mary Rose*, constructed at Portsmouth in 1510. The town's defences at Portsmouth were also improved. The installation of a military garrison in the town was the start of a long

Harbour and these were followed by other castles at Sandown, Yarmouth, Netley and Hamble.

Portsmouth and the Isle of Wight were the targets of a major French seaborne attack in 1545, in retaliation for the English capture of Boulogne in 1544. A fleet of 225 ships and thousands of men arrived off the island in July 1545. Henry VIII marshalled a large fleet and army at Portsmouth, and a major battle was threatened, although never actually took place. The worst single incident of the campaign was the tragic loss of the *Mary Rose*, which capsized and sank on 19 July as she sailed out to fight

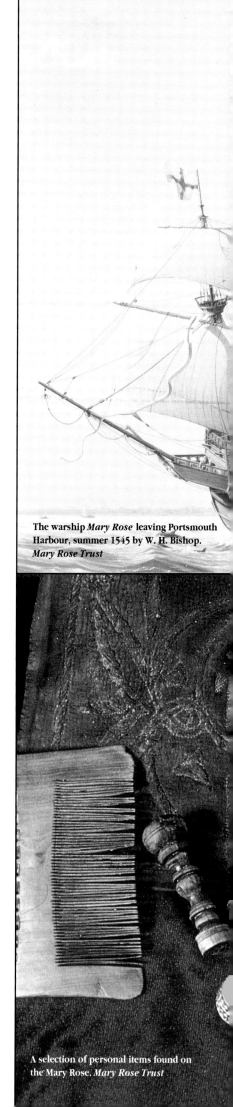

The warship *Mary Rose* leaving Portsmouth Harbour, summer 1545 by W. H. Bishop. *Mary Rose Trust*

Aerial view of Southsea Castle.

tradition which was to survive until the second half of the 20th century.

Henry VIII continued the policy of favouring Portsmouth, and he needed to, having upset the Catholic powers of France and Spain, with his declaration of independence from the Pope. He appointed commissioners to 'search and defend' the coastline. A chain of castles and blockhouses from the Scottish border round to Pembrokeshire resulted, with the defence of the Solent being of prime concern.

Castles were built first (in 1539-40) at Calshot and Hurst to protect Southampton Water, with blockhouses at East and West Cowes. In 1544 Southsea Castle was built to protect the deep channel approaches to Portsmouth

the French. As many as 700 men may have been drowned.

Portsmouth dockyard declined in importance after the reign of Henry VIII, and later suffered serious fires. The growing threat from Spain and the Spanish Netherlands, from the 1570s onwards, meant that other dockyards on the Thames, and the naval base at Chatham, had more strategic significance. Portsmouth dockyard was to play little part in England's long sea war with Spain (1585-1603).

However, the defences of the city of Portsmouth were repaired and modernised in Elizabeth I's time, to give a clear line of fire from the walls. This can still be seen in the open spaces around Old Portsmouth.

A selection of personal items found on the Mary Rose. *Mary Rose Trust*

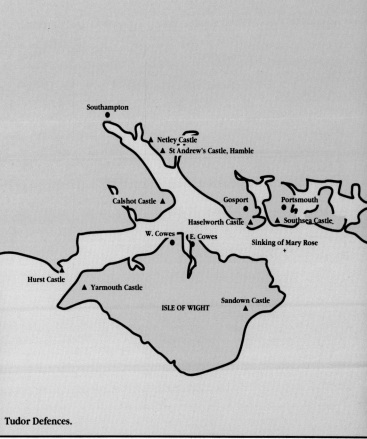

Tudor Defences.

**3 CALSHOT CASTLE**
This example of an early Tudor Castle (as completed 1540) shows the traditional rounded style, replaced only a few years later by the angular style such as at Southsea. *English Heritage*

**4 YARMOUTH CASTLE**
One of the later, angular Tudor designs, this castle was not one of Henry's original choices for a site, but when the French landed on the Isle of Wight in 1545 he changed his mind.

**1 SOUTHSEA CASTLE**
Henry VIII built the castle overlooking the deep water channel approaching Portsmouth Harbour in 1544. Captured in the Civil War, accidentally blown up in the 18th century and re-equipped in the 19th century, it has had an eventful history.

**2 HURST CASTLE**
A dramatic setting on a spit in the narrow western approaches to the Solent, makes this Tudor castle a worthwhile visit. Built between 1541 and 1544 it has been considerably extended since. *English Heritage*

**5 MARY ROSE**
In 1982 the hull of Henry VIII's famous warship was lifted from the seabed and returned to a dry dock in Portsmouth, where she was built. She is now on display with nearly 2,000 objects recovered from the ship. *Mary Rose Trust*

# THE CIVIL WAR

 T THE BEGINNING of the 17th century James I made peace with Spain, put a stop to privateering and neglected the Navy. Even Henry VII's dry dock was filled with rubble in 1623.

During the reign of Charles I Portsmouth saw a revival of activity, although the Thames dockyards continued to be favoured. Charles knew the town well though, returning there in October 1623, with his friend George Villiers, Duke of Buckingham, after unsuccessfully attempting to woo the Spanish Infanta in Madrid (later a bust of Charles was erected on the Square Tower in commemoration of this). However, in 1628, the immensely unpopular Buckingham returned there to fit out an expedition for the relief of Huguenots in La Rochelle, but was murdered in his lodgings (now 11 High Street) by a discontented ex-army officer.

The issue of raising funds for such expeditions, through a Ship Tax, was one of the key issues in growing national discontent, leading to the split between Charles I and his Parliament, and then the Civil War.

When Civil War did break out in 1642, the Navy declared for Parliament, but the Governor of Portsmouth, Colonel George Goring, declared for King Charles, despite having earlier pledged allegiance to Parliament. Goring had already acquired large sums of money from both the King and Parliament for work on the town's defences.

Colonel Goring tried to hold the town for the King but with little support from the townspeople. After bombardment from Gosport, a naval blockade and the taking of Southsea Castle, the garrison surrendered in 1642.

By 1643 Hampshire had become very much a frontline county between the Royalist-held West Country and the Parliament-controlled south-east. Frequent skirmishes took place between the opposing sides and a

was not so. He was lodged at Carisbrooke Castle, politely at first, with visits by the local gentry – even a stay with Sir John Oglander at Nunwell was allowed. Very soon he became more and more of a prisoner for fear of an attempt to liberate him. With more Parliamentary Commissioners and soldiers coming over from the mainland, there was increasing trouble between islanders and the troops. The King was therefore taken back across the Solent, where he stayed three weeks in a small cell in Hurst Castle before being taken back to London for his eventual execution in 1649.

It was during Charles I's time on the island that two forts were added to the Portsmouth harbour defences, with Fort Charles on the shore at Gosport and Fort James on Rat Island. However it was the appointment of a Navy Commissioner, Colonel William Willoughby, at Portsmouth in 1649 that led to a major revival of the dockyard. A dozen new ships were built between 1650 and 1658 and a core of resident shipwrights and dockyard

The house in Old Portsmouth where the Duke of Buckingham was murdered in 1628.

The Bust of King Charles I, inset in Square Tower, Old Portsmouth.

major battle took place at Cheriton near Alresford in spring 1644 which, for the first time, put the King on the defensive.

Lord Hopton's defeated royal army fell back on Basing House, the home of the Marquis of Winchester, which had become one of the main royalist strongholds in the Kingdom. This great Tudor house had already survived one siege and in the following summer was to suffer two more before finally being stormed by Oliver Cromwell in person on 14 October 1645.

After five years of unsuccessful Civil War, the King was in Army Custody at Hampton Court, when on 11 November 1647, he escaped. He fled to the Isle of Wight, thinking that the Governor would support him, but this

workers was established. Although the outbreak of wars against the Dutch led to a concentration of activity in the Thames and Medway ports, Portsmouth was a valuable repair and building yard with Gosport increasingly used as a victualling centre.

The Dutch wars did impinge on the area in February 1653 when Admiral Blake fought against the Dutch Admiral Van Tromp off the Isle of Wight and 1,000 Dutch prisoners were brought back to Southampton.

In 1659, with its support of Sir Arthur Hesilrige, Portsmouth was the first place in England to rebel against a military government and so played a significant part in events which culminated in the restoration of Charles II.

**Carisbrooke Castle, Isle of Wight.**
*English Heritage*

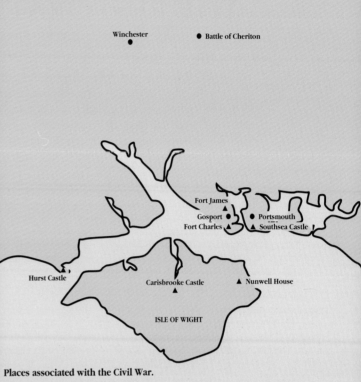

Siege of Basing House ▲

Winchester ● ● Battle of Cheriton

Fort James ▲
Gosport ● ● Portsmouth
Fort Charles ▲ ▲ Southsea Castle

Hurst Castle

Carisbrooke Castle ▲ ▲ Nunwell House

ISLE OF WIGHT

**Places associated with the Civil War.**

1

## 1        NUNWELL HOUSE

In beautiful surroundings just west of Brading on the Isle of Wight, this house was home to the Oglander family for many years and it acted as a base for repelling potential French, Dutch, Spanish and German invasions. King Charles I spent his last night here before close confinement in Carisbrooke Castle.

## 2        BASING HOUSE

The ruins of Basing House, near Basingstoke, which was destroyed by Oliver Cromwell in 1645 after a year's siege, are the scene of annual re-enactments of this Civil War battle.

# THE RESTORATION

ITH HIS RESTORATION to the throne in 1660, Charles II soon started on a programme of developing the dockyard in Portsmouth and establishing it as the prime naval port in the country. He was undoubtedly conscious of the role it had played in the fate of his father, and as an important 'gateway' throughout history. It was at the Sally Port in Portsmouth that Catherine of Braganza was to arrive in 1662 for her wedding to Charles. She was taken the short distance to the Domus Dei, which was the Governor's residence and where the marriage ceremony took place.

In 1664 the Duke of York and Albany's Maritime Regiment was created. Known as Marines, they became Royal Marines in 1804. The navy became the Royal Navy in 1670.

Samuel Pepys, as Clerk of the Acts of the King's Ships, was involved in the reorganisation of the dockyard, and the King's patronage of the Royal Society encouraged new developments in navigation and cartography.

Just as important for Portsmouth as the development of the dockyard, was the arrival in 1665 of Sir Bernard de Gomme, 'Chief Engineer of all the King's Castles in England and Wales', with instructions to strengthen Portsmouth's defences. Added impetus to these orders came in 1667 with a daring Dutch raid on the Medway ports and the loss of *The Royal Charles*, taken as their

involving many of its inhabitants, with brewhouses, ropemakers, clothiers and lodging houses.

As in earlier times, periods of prosperity for the naval towns did not necessarily coincide with those for the trading port. In 1683 the Mayor of Southampton wrote to the Secretary of State:

'Southampton has been a rich place, but is now quite the contrary. The late rebellion (ie the Civil War) despoiled this chamber of all public moneys, in the plague 1,700 inhabitants died, the Dutch war robbed them of almost all their ships. The public revenues are

A south-easterly view of Portsmouth's Fortifications in 1765 by John Walters. *Portsmouth City Museums*

prize. Working over a 20-year period, with Dutch prisoners brought from Portchester Castle as the workforce, Sir Bernard transformed the fortifications. The main lessons of the Civil War were the strengthening of Southsea Castle; the securing of the Portsbridge crossing and the need to cover the shipping channels with artillery.

On the Gosport side of the harbour ramparts and a moat were constructed, together with a new fort at the harbour entrance. This was Fort Blockhouse, which can still be seen among the more modern buildings of HMS *Dolphin*, the Submarine Base. Although these were primarily constructed to prevent bombardment of Portsmouth, Gosport was itself becoming increasingly important with the victualling and manning of ships

incredibly sunk, by which the Corporation is under great difficulties to discharge the burden on the chamber and the great rent to the King, as also repairing the walls, bulwarks, quays and seabanks.'

It was after the Restoration of the Monarchy that the country first had an established army although a number of regiments can trace their origins back to even earlier times.

A succession of infantry and cavalry regiments were raised for campaigns, chiefly in Europe. Whilst they are now known by their county titles, they were originally known by the name of their commanding officer. For example, the Royal Hampshire Regiment, which was raised in 1702, was known as Thomas Meredith's Regiment of Foot.

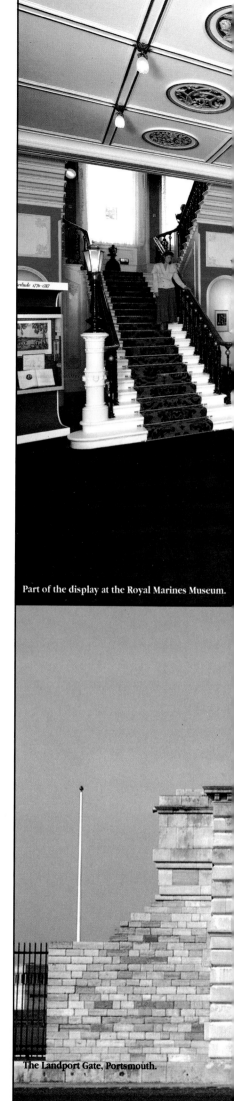

Part of the display at the Royal Marines Museum.

The Landport Gate, Portsmouth.

An outline of Portsmouth and Gosport Fortifications.

**1 ROYAL MARINES MUSEUM**
Situated within the splendour of a Victorian Officers' Mess at Southsea, this museum tells a huge story spanning over 300 years in a mixture of traditional and hi-tech display methods. Highlights include 18th century life at sea, Trafalgar, Jutland, the Commandos, the Falklands conflict and Arctic warfare.

**2 ROYAL BARGE**
The state barge of King Charles II is on display in the Royal Naval Museum, Portsmouth. The oldest barge in existence, it was also used in January 1806 to carry Nelson's body in his great funeral procession.

# THE 18th CENTURY
# WARS WITH FRANCE

T HE PROTESTANT William of Orange was brought to the throne in 1688 and attention shifted back to Catholic France instead of the Dutch. Portsmouth harbour again benefited from its geographical proximity to France, which was to be the nation's main enemy for the next 130 years, with seven major confrontations between 1688 and 1815.

One of the main features of the first phase of construction in this period is still evident in the boundary wall of the dockyard, and the main gate, still in use today. Dockyard workers soon started building houses on the common land between the town and the dockyard.

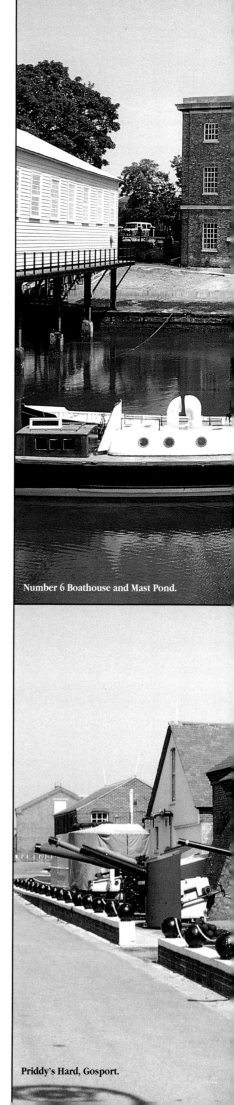

The narrow strip of land at the entrance to the harbour, known as Point, had also developed quickly early in the century but this was outside the jurisdiction of the town itself and it became notorious as a place of relaxation for sailors. By 1716 it had many brothels and over 40 beerhouses, coffee and brandy shops.

In 1723 the dockyard was expanded northwards, with brick-built offices, houses, ropewalks and workshops replacing earlier wooden buildings. By 1775 2,500 men were employed there.

Portsmouth itself also grew, with a new town hall, grammar school, theatre, banks and a bathing house built on the Point. In the 1770s the town's magazine was removed from the Square Tower and transferred to a new building at Priddy's Hard on the Gosport side of the harbour.

Gosport was also the site for a major extension to the Haslar Hospital and a victualling establishment, the appropriately named Weevil Yard.

the entrance to Langstone Harbour and Eastney Beach was covered by Eastney and Lumps Batteries. In 1770 ramparts and moats encircling the town of Portsea started.

Gosport defences were also extended southwards (where they can still be seen) and northwards to enclose Priddy's Hard, with Fort Monckton built to protect the exposed beaches to the west.

The need for a larger fleet at this time kept the dockyard busy, and there was also a growth in commercial shipyards all around the Solent, notably in the River Hamble and at Buckler's Hard.

Of 27 new ships commissioned for the Navy by William III four were built at Bursledon, on the River Hamble, by William Wyatt in the 1690s. The site fell out of favour and no commercial naval shipbuilding took place in Hampshire between 1698 and 1740. Two of his master shipbuilders, Philemon Ewer and Moody Janverin carried on in the 1740s, but George Parsons revived activity when he leased a site below the Jolly Sailor public house.

Number 6 Boathouse and Mast Pond.

**Portsmouth harbour looking South around 1790 by Capt Robert Elliott, RN.** *Portsmouth City Museums*

The national strategic importance of Portsmouth Harbour was confirmed when Portsmouth and Gosport became the only towns to be newly fortified on a large scale during the 18th century. In particuar the Jacobite Rebellion of 1745 caused much alarm, with fear of French assistance involving a raid on the south coast. The engineers had to widen the scope of their defensive schemes because mobile artillery raised fears of an enemy landing on an undefended part of the south coast and advancing on Portsmouth overland.

By the end of the century, the whole of Portsea Island was defended from attack from the north by the Hilsea Lines. At Portsbridge Fort the only road entrance on to the island was re-fortified. Fort Cumberland was built to protect

The most renowned ship from there was the *Elephant,* on board which Nelson put the telescope to his blind eye at the Battle of Copenhagen. The yard eventually shifted to Warsash, but between 1650 and 1814 a total of 51 naval ships had been built on the Hamble.

The Beaulieu River in the New Forest had been the site of plans in 1720 for a new town for importing sugar cane. Despite the failure of the project, the site at Buckler's Hard had been used for exporting timber from the forest, and in 1745 the Wyatt brothers won a naval contract to build the *Surprise.* Of those ships built there between 1745 and 1827 most were built under the direction of the Adams family, including three of Nelson's Trafalgar fleet, including one of his favourite ships *Agamemnon.*

Priddy's Hard, Gosport.

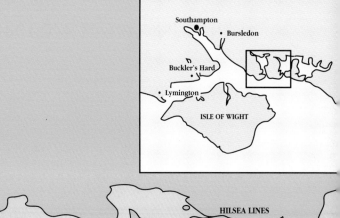

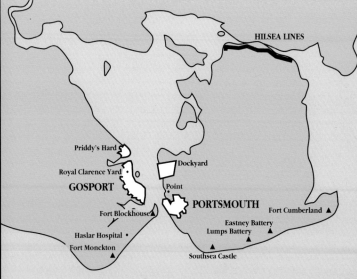

The 18th Century Defences of Portsmouth and Gosport.

Map labels:
Southampton
Bursledon
Buckler's Hard
Lymington
ISLE OF WIGHT

HILSEA LINES
Priddy's Hard
Royal Clarence Yard
GOSPORT
Dockyard
Point
PORTSMOUTH
Fort Blockhouse
Fort Cumberland
Eastney Battery
Lumps Battery
Haslar Hospital
Fort Monckton
Southsea Castle

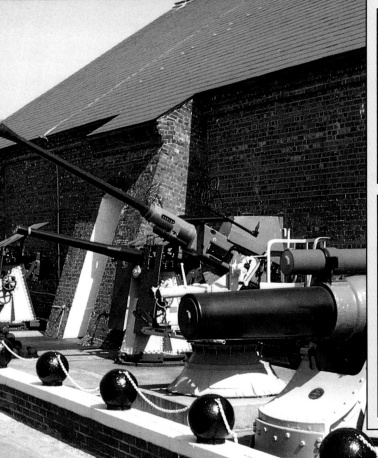

1    BUCKLER'S HARD
The museum tells the story of shipbuilding at Buckler's Hard including three ships for Nelson's fleet. There are also reconstructed 18th century cottage interiors and a display of 18th century life.

2    PORTSMOUTH DOCKYARD
The historic area of Portsmouth dockyard with its fine Georgian storehouses, boathouses, mast ponds and ropehouses is as much a reminder of Britain's military past as any castles or ships. It was also one of the country's main industrial centres in the 18th century.

# THE NAPOLEONIC WARS

 URING THE GREAT French Wars (1793-1815) the British Navy maintained vigilance around the world. It attempted to prevent the French fleet from supporting their land forces, and particularly from gaining control of the Channel, which would be essential if they were to fulfil their plans for invading Britain. Portsmouth's role as a principal naval port was thus intensified.

In 1797 the first steam engine was installed in the dockyard and a few years later Marc Isambard Brunel introduced his revolutionary system for the speedier manufacture of ships' pulley blocks. These 'block mills' still stand in the dockyard.

Vice-Admiral Lord Nelson, by Beechey.

It was in 1805 that Nelson embarked from Portsmouth before the Battle of Trafalgar. As cheering crowds prevented him from leaving The George where he had breakfasted, he used a back door and side alley. He was spotted, quickly surrounded and had to press his way through the throng to the beach near the Round Tower. Eleven weeks later HMS *Victory* lay at Spithead with the body of Lord Nelson on board.

After Napoleon's defeats in 1814 and 1815, Portsmouth was the scene of the country's greatest celebrations. The population of the town trebled. The route from Portsdown Hill to the Governor's House in Old Portsmouth was lined with 11,000 infantry, dragoons and militia. Four days of celebrations included a Review of the Fleet and inspections of the troops and dockyard, itself already a great visitor attraction.

Soon French prisoners-of-war were leaving the hulks

skirmishers and snipers. These soon became an elite corps of three battalions under Major General John Moore, in the Peninsular Wars in Spain. The Duke of Wellington thought them to be 'the flower of the Army, the finest infantry in the world'. It was in the Peninsular War that the Duke of Wellington had risen from being the youngest Lt-General in the army (1808) to being Duke by 1814. He added sound tactics to this new organisation, and after securing a string of famous victories in the Peninsular War, his army played the greater part in Napoleon's final defeat at Waterloo on 18 June 1815.

It was during this period that two voluntary forces were raised. Following a proposal by Sir William Pitt in 1794, some counties raised complete regiments, whilst generally the organisation was at a more local level of troop or squadron. Many units were disbanded after the Peace of Amiens in 1801 but when war broke out again

**Portsmouth Point. Engraving after Thomas Rowlandson, c1800.** *Portsmouth City Museums*

in the harbour and Portchester Castle. Events, though, were interrupted by Napoleon's escape from Elba and the Waterloo campaign.

Waterloo was to be a major test for the newly reorganised army. The Duke of York, Commander-in-Chief since 1795, had reformed the numerous independent brigades into Divisions and reorganised the support services. The later successes of the Army in the Napoleonic Wars owed much to his improvements in military systems especially in training and discipline and the drill for infantry and cavalry. It was in 1797 that he obtained an Act for the 60th Royal Americans to wear a green jacket. In 1800, when the experimental Corps of Riflemen were formed, they dressed in green. (The descendants of these regiments are The Royal Green Jackets.) These green-jacketed troops were used in the front of the Army as

in 1803 they were hurriedly re-enrolled. In 1804 an Act was passed creating a Volunteer Force to provide a large number of non-regular troops to defend the country against an invasion by a 150,000 strong French army mustered at Boulogne. No invasion took place and the volunteers were stood down after Waterloo.

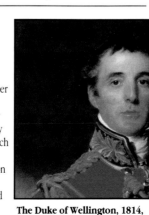

**The Duke of Wellington, 1814, by Sir Thomas Lawrence.**

HMS *Victory*, launched in 1765, at Portsmouth Naval Base.

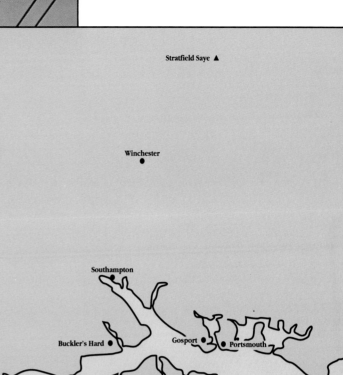

Stratfield Saye ▲

Winchester
●

Southampton
●

Buckler's Hard ●

Gosport ● ● Portsmouth

ISLE OF WIGHT

**Hampshire during the Napoleonic Wars.**

1   ROYAL NAVAL MUSEUM AND
HMS *VICTORY*
The museum covers the whole history
of the Navy from the Romans to the
Gulf. The museum also has many relics
and exhibits about Nelson and HMS
*Victory* in the Victory Gallery
(pictured) and elsewhere in the
museum.

2      STRATFIELD SAYE
Built in the reign of Charles I, the
house has been the home of the Dukes
of Wellington since it was presented to
the Great Duke in 1817. A Wellington
Exhibition takes you back to scenes
from his life and the historic Battle of
Waterloo.

3 ROYAL GREEN JACKETS MUSEUM
One of the highlights of this museum
in Winchester is an impressive diorama
of the Battle of Waterloo which
contains some 25,000 model soldiers.
There is also the opportunity to fire the
Baker Rifle, used by the ancestors of
the Green Jackets during the
Peninsular War and Battle of Waterloo.
This museum tells its Regiment's story
from 1741 until the present day.

# THE CRIMEAN WAR AND THE CAMP AT ALDERSHOT

AVAL PRIORITIES AFTER the Napoleonic wars returned to protecting the country's flourishing trade interest as peace brought increasing prosperity to Southampton and the growth of ports such as Bristol and Liverpool. However, the Navy needed fewer ships and men for its tasks and there was little work in Portsmouth Dockyard. Inevitably a vast number of soldiers were discharged from the Army and there was great unemployment throughout the county leading to considerable unrest including riots in Portsmouth.

As the country, and Europe, gradually settled down to a long period of peace, the various settlements on Portsea Island continued to grow and Southsea expanded as a residential area for servicemen and retired dockyard officials.

The Duke of Wellington remained an immensely influential figure and when not in political office he had, since 1818, held the two great military appointments of state, Master General of the Ordnance and Commander-in-Chief, the latter until the day of his death in 1852. Although he had, during the 1840s, drawn attention to the inadequacy of the country's defences, little was done until the year of Revolutions in Europe, 1848, and the return of Napoleon's nephew to France convinced the government of a real threat from across the channel.

Accordingly, in 1852 work was begun on Fort Elson and Fort Gomer, to the west of Gosport, following the theory that the dockyard was vulnerable to forces landing nearby and bombarding it from inland. The dockyard itself was adjusting to the new requirements of steamships in the Royal Navy, and four new docks and a steam basin were added.

It was the Prince Consort who finally was to persuade the new Commander-in-Chief, Lord Hardinge, that something needed to be done to improve the training of

southwards and so they went to the aid of Turkey when it was invaded. The Russians soon withdrew from the disputed territory but the Allies decided upon a punitive operation to capture the port of Sebastopol in the Crimea believing this would take about six weeks.

The war had started with appropriate splendour when the Queen reviewed the fleet before it left Portsmouth in 1854, but a chaotic campaign ensued and with uncoordinated leadership, endless inter-allied disputes, supply failures and enormous casualties from disease, the war dragged on for two years.

To replace the regular soldiers sent to the Crimea the Militia was called up, but there was a public outcry when it was proposed that they should be billeted on the local population. So although Aldershot was originally intended to be only a summer tented camp it was decided to build two wooden hutted camps there to house twenty thousand men, a figure later reduced to twelve thousand.

It was clearly in the Prince Consort's mind that Aldershot should become a great centre for the Army as no

Married quarters, Rifle Brigade, Aldershot 1886.

the Army. While holding a training camp for two months on Chobham Common in the summer of 1853 Lord Hardinge rode over the heathland around Aldershot and Farnborough and in February 1854 10,000 acres of heathland were purchased to serve as a summer training area for both the regular army and the militia. Within two months of the purchase Britain and France had gone to war with Russia in the Crimea. This coincidence was to herald a century of almost continuous change in the fighting services and led to Aldershot becoming the 'Home of the British Army'.

Aldershot was a convenient location from which to deploy troops to the south coast in the event of French invasion but at this juncture Britain and France were more concerned to stop Russia expanding its empire

sooner were the huts erected than he was writing to the Commander-in-Chief enjoining him 'to put permanent barracks on the land and the country will never be allowed to sell it ..... The state of popular feeling engendered by the war is such that you can ask Parliament for anything you want. Strike while the iron is hot.'

Whilst the hutted camps were being built the Prince Consort also arranged the building of a small Royal Pavilion where he and the Queen could stay while visiting the army and this was first occupied by the Monarch in April 1856 when she reviewed the Militia prior to their disbanding at the end of the war.

However, no Royal Review could disguise the military incompetence revealed in the Crimea where the medical services were found to be the most neglected and

Re-enactment at Royal Victoria Country Park.

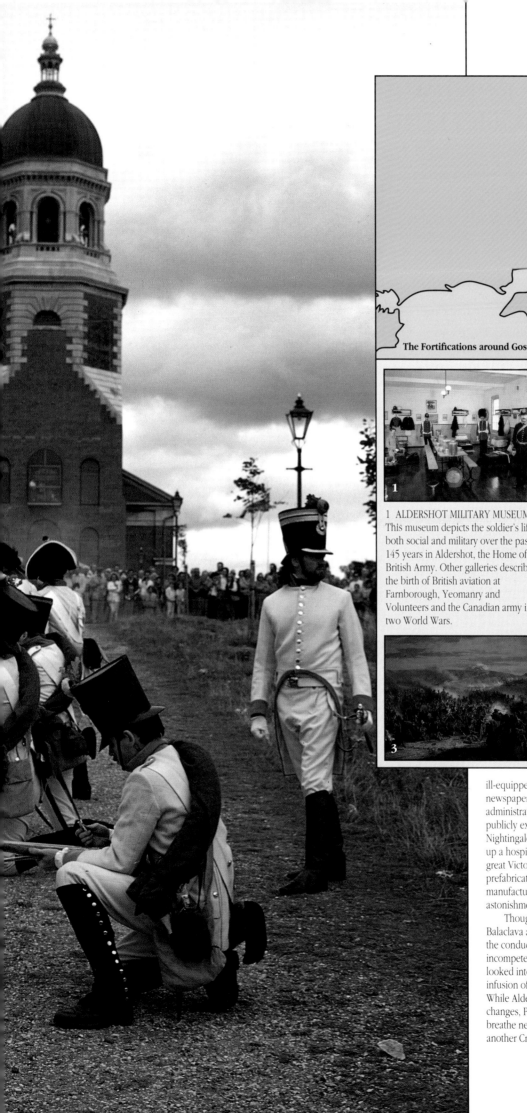

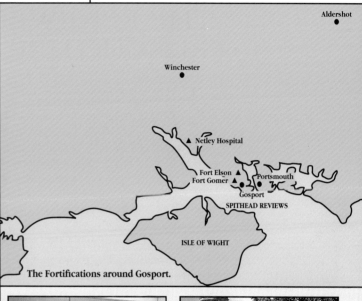

The Fortifications around Gosport.

**1  ALDERSHOT MILITARY MUSEUM**
This museum depicts the soldier's life, both social and military over the past 145 years in Aldershot, the Home of the British Army. Other galleries describe the birth of British aviation at Farnborough, Yeomanry and Volunteers and the Canadian army in two World Wars.

**2 ROYAL VICTORIA COUNTRY PARK**
The park occupies the grounds of what was once the British Army's principal military hospital built after the Crimean War. All that remains of the building is the Chapel which now houses a fascinating heritage centre and offers splendid views along Southampton Water.

**3   ROYAL HUSSARS MUSEUM**
The history of the 10th and 11th Hussars from 1715 to the present day covers many famous events from our military past. The Crimean War and the two World Wars are strongly featured in the museum in Winchester.

ill-equipped of all. Being the first war reported by a newspaper correspondent, many of the problems of administration and the dreadful toll of sickness were publicly exposed and this eventually led to Florence Nightingale and 38 nurses being asked to go out and set up a hospital at Scutari near Constantinople. Brunel, the great Victorian engineer, was commissioned to provide a prefabricated wooden hospital which he designed, manufactured and despatched within three months, to the astonishment of the War Office.

Though the names Sebastopol, Alma, Inkerman and Balaclava are treasured battle honours of many regiments, the conduct of the fighting soldier could not disguise the incompetence of the system. A commission of inquiry looked into the Army's supply services and began an infusion of new life into a creaking military organisation. While Aldershot was to be the chief witness to these changes, Palmerston – the Prime Minister – was soon to breathe new life into the defence of Portsmouth where another Crimean victory review had been held in 1856.

# THE RENEWED FRENCH THREAT

 HE ALLIANCE WITH FRANCE, following the Crimean War, did not last long and there were several invasion scares during the 1850s. Both popular and official concern were heightened by technological changes in military and naval equipment. Not only did France build a new type of ironclad steam-powered warship *La Gloire* in 1859, but also extended the important naval dockyard at Cherbourg, aimed, it seemed, at Portsmouth and the heart of England. Moreover France had a much larger army than Britain.

The British response to the perceived French threat was firstly, to update the Navy, our traditional defence. HMS *Warrior* (1860) was the splendid result. Secondly, the British felt the need to protect important ports and dockyards, of which Portsmouth was the chief, by sea-facing batteries and mutually supporting forts which would be built or modernised to provide a defence ring and manned by mixed detachments of regular soldiers, militia and volunteers.

Various proposals for improved fortifications around Portsmouth were made during the 1850s, and the Gosport Line, of which Fort Brockhurst is an example, was begun. An important technological development, the rifling of gun barrels to increase offensive range, became a practical proposition during the 1850s. This raised the question of the siting of forts to protect Portsmouth, Gosport and the

resign three times as Chancellor. If necessary, as Palmerston wrote to the Queen, it was better to lose Mr Gladstone than to lose Portsmouth.

So, despite the plans being reduced in scale, many new forts and batteries were built around Portsmouth and Gosport, including a line of six forts on Portsdown Hill, overlooking Portsmouth and Gosport, and some remarkable steel and granite sea

The Portsdown Volunteers firing a mortar at Fort Nelson.

Needles Battery.

Isle of Wight.

All these considerations were examined in detail by a special Royal Commission, whose secretary was Major William (later Sir) Drummond Jervois RE, Assistant Inspector-General of Fortifications. The Royal Commission reported in 1860, recommending the most extensive scheme of fortifications ever undertaken in peacetime with Portsmouth the first of nine vital naval and military centres to be considered. Enthusiastically adopted by Lord Palmerston, the Prime Minister, the scheme nevertheless had to be trimmed due to political opposition and Gladstone threatened to

forts to defend Spithead.

The Isle of Wight was incorporated into the scheme of Portsmouth's defences for the first time since Tudor times, and more forts and batteries were built on the island.

Many of these forts were subsequently adapted to incorporate changes in artillery, and to serve in two World Wars, but these were the last self contained and self defensible fortresses to be built in this country. That many of them never fired a gun in anger can either be taken as a sign of their success as a deterrent, or a measure of Palmerston's Folly.

HMS *Warrior* 1860, at Portsmouth Naval Base.
*Warrior Preservation Trust*

**ISLE OF WIGHT**

Horse Sand Fort
No Man's Land Fort
Fort Albert  Fort Victoria  Puckpool Battery
Warden Point  St. Helens Fort
Battery  Cliff End Battery
Golden Hill Fort
Hatherwood Point  Bembridge Fort  Redcliff Battery
Needles  Battery  Yaverland
Sandown Fort
Barrack Battery

Fort Nelson  Fort Southwick  Fort Widley  Fort Purbrook
Fort Wallington
Farlington Redoubt

Fort Fareham

Hilsea
Lines

Fort Elson

Fort Brockhurst

Fort Rowner

Fort Grange

Fort Gomer

Stokes Bay
Line
Browndown Battery  Spitbank Fort

Gilkicker Fort

**Portsmouth Harbour and Solent Fortifications.**

| 1 | FORT PURBROOK | 3 | SPITBANK FORT | All these forts, Fort Nelson, Needles |
|---|---|---|---|---|
| 2 | FORT BROCKHURST | 4 | GOLDEN HILL FORT | Battery and HMS *Warrior* 1860 are |
|   | *English Heritage* | 5 | NOTHE FORT Weymouth, Dorset | open to the public. |

23

# THE CLIMAX OF EMPIRE

 HE THREATENED INVASION did not take place and in fact the years following 1860 were to see the town of Portsmouth put on a more peaceful air with the rapid growth of Southsea as a resort. The Dockyard was not idle though, and during the 1860s it adapted all the facilities associated with the building of sailing ships so they could meet the requirements of steamships. By 1864 its total area had increased to 260 acres, when even further extensions were begun.

When the army returned from the Crimea they went to Aldershot rather than being dispersed in small detachments in castles, forts, billets and county towns as had been the previous pattern. The 'Division at Aldershot' rose from four infantry battalions in 1856 to 24 battalions and three cavalry regiments in 1896. Such a force, with its artillery and engineers required a permanent supply and administrative organisation to support it, leading to the provision of hospitals, schools, churches, a military police force, butchery, bakery and so on. With 17,000 soldiers and 6,000 horses the camp at Aldershot was to become the first complete military town built in the Kingdom since the Roman occupation.

It was also a period of major technological transition. In the Navy, wooden, three-deck sailing ships with muzzle-loading guns were replaced by armour-plated steam ships with turreted breech-loading guns. Gunnery became a new science. Its first school had been established on board HMS *Excellent* in Portsmouth harbour in 1830, initiating the ranges still in use towards Portchester and Fareham. It expanded and moved on to Whale Island in 1864, and moved ashore completely in 1891.

In 1876 HMS *Vernon* became separated from HMS *Excellent* and pioneered work on torpedoes from its berth at Gunwharf just south of the Harbour Station. Whilst Fort Albert, on the Isle of Wight, was a base for testing the Brennan, an early type of torpedo.

waterfront, meanwhile had grown from its original storage magazine and now had new laboratory rooms where shells and cartridges were filled. By 1903 increased storage needs for explosives meant an expansion further up the Gosport shore to Bedenham. Elsewhere in the area older fortifications were used for a variety of experiments in new technology and Hurst Castle was the site of an ingenious plan to overcome the threat of enemy forces using the Isle of Wight as an invasion base by digging a tunnel across to Yarmouth.

While the Army's overseas commitments continued from the Indian Mutiny through the Chinese, Zulu and Afghan Wars, many reforms were instituted particularly those of Edward Cardwell during Gladstone's first ministry (1865-74). Recruiting was improved, flogging abolished in

The Grand Naval Review at Spithead, 1853.
*Portsmouth City Museums*

HMS *Dreadnought* in 1909. *Royal Naval Museum*

Just across the water at Gosport's Fort Blockhouse, HMS *Dolphin* was established as the home of the submarine service in 1905. *Holland 1*, the Navy's first submarine, was one of the boats based there. Nearby is the Admiralty Research Establishment, founded in the 1880s, to enable the scientist 'Eddy' Froude to continue his father's pioneering work on the testing of new ship designs by the use of models. The original 400ft tank is still used.

Herbert E. Vosper established his firm in Old Portsmouth in 1870 while the Haslar Gunboat Yards, in Gosport, launched gunboats down its slipways from a mechanical cradle which ran along in front of a dozen or so separate ship-building sheds; a very early example of the factory principle applied to ships.

Priddy's Hard, further north on the Gosport

peacetime, purchase of commissions forbidden, breech loading rifles introduced and the infantry reorganised on a county basis.

If any particular date can be given to the Climax of Empire it must surely be 1897, the year of Queen Victoria's Diamond Jubilee. Britannia ruled the waves, the Empire's extent was at its greatest and the Queen's family were married into most of the royal families of Europe. At Aldershot the Queen reviewed 30,000 troops, including contingents from throughout the empire, but soon the country was again at war – with the army again unprepared for the conditions of mobile warfare with the Boers in a country so vast as South Africa.

Serious reverses in the early stages of the war led to a demand for more 'mounted infantry'. A school for their

*Holland 1* in Portsmouth Harbour.
*Submarine Museum*

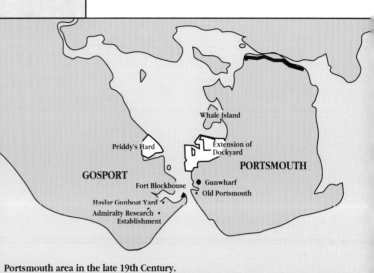

Portsmouth area in the late 19th Century.

**1 ROYAL NAVY SUBMARINE MUSEUM**
The key attractions at this Gosport Museum are HMS *Alliance*, a World War II period craft and *Holland 1*, Britain's first submarine, which had sunk in 1913 to be raised again in 1982.

**2    GURKHA MUSEUM**
The remarkable story of how these mountain people from Nepal have provided front line troops for the British Army since 1815, is told in this new museum located in the Peninsula Barracks, Winchester.

training was established at Aldershot and the Imperial Yeomanry was formed from county Yeomanry Regiments. Volunteer Regiments offered their services and the War Office authorised the despatch of one volunteer company to every battalion serving in South Africa.

So the start of the 20th century saw major reforms being required again in both the Navy and the Army. Admiral 'Jacky' Fisher, First Sea Lord, reformed and rearmed the Navy, with 1906 seeing the launch of the 17,000-ton *Dreadnought* at Portsmouth. Eighteen of this class were laid down between 1905 and 1910.

The Army, which had sent units out to South Africa piecemeal, was at last organised into permanent fighting formations of brigades and divisions with their own artillery, engineers, medical and support services. This required the building of a series of new camps and barracks at Blackdown, Ewshott, Longmoor and Bordon.

At the same time, the recent inventions of the internal combustion engine and the electric generator were to start a technological revolution in the fighting services, the scope of which was unimaginable at the time.

All these reforms and inventions were to be tested before long in a period when Hampshire – with Portsmouth, Gosport, Aldershot and Farnborough, being closely involved with such new developments – was once again at the forefront of the Defence of the Realm.

# THE GREAT WAR

 HE PERIOD UP TO 1914 was to see an increased pace of technological development and rearmament which was to influence all parts of the Defence of the Realm area, but none more so than at Farnborough.

As early as 1862, Lieutenant Grover of the Royal Engineers began experiments with balloons and kites as a means of improving artillery observation. By 1880 man-carrying balloons were used by the army on manoeuvres at Aldershot, balloon detachments were sent on overseas campaigns and in 1890 the Balloon Section of the Royal Engineers moved from Chatham to Aldershot to be the ancestor of the Air Battalion, the Royal Flying Corps and ultimately the RAF.

In 1901 Samuel Franklin Cody, an inventive American, had been drawn across the Channel in a canoe attached to one of his large box kites, and in 1903 he had demonstrated their value for gunnery observation to the Navy at Whale Island, Portsmouth. By 1906 he was 'Chief Instructor in Kiting' at the Balloon School, Aldershot. The first military airship, *Nulli Secundus* flew from Farnborough to London in 1907 and their minds turned to powered flight.

Cody's experiments with kites were to lead to the real breakthrough in aeronautical developments and learning from the experience of the Wright brothers, he achieved the first officialy recognised aeroplane flight in Great Britain in October 1908 at Farnborough, in 'British Army Aeroplane No 1'.

Within four years, on 13 April 1912, the Air Battalion Royal Engineers became the Royal Flying Corps and by October 1912 the RFC Naval Wing was formed with its first station at Calshot Castle, the Tudor castle at the

dominion solidarity, Colonel Sir Henry Pellat brought his battalion of volunteers, the Queens Own Rifles of Canada, over to Aldershot entirely at his own expense to take part in the autumn manoeuvres.

At the outbreak of war in 1914 the divisions in Aldershot Command became the spearhead of the British Expeditionary Force to France. The barracks they vacated were filled by thousands of volunteers flocking to the colours, while battalions of enthusiastic but completely untrained Canadians crossed the Atlantic to occupy camps in Salisbury Plain and around Longmoor and Bordon.

The first few months of war were to provide important new lessons for both services. The impact of torpedoes and submarines was felt with the loss of three cruisers in the North Sea in the first months of the war to German submarines. The Battle of Ypres in

Samuel Cody.

Cody's first flight at Farnborough.

entrance to Southampton Water. Its first commander commuted daily from Southsea in his own plane. For the Spithead Review in July 1914 the base was able to provide 17 aircraft for a fly past, and, even more important, it dropped the first torpedo from an aircraft on 28 July. This review showed the Royal Navy at the peak of its power (with 68 battleships, 218 destroyers and 76 submarines on show) at a time when the country was preparing for war. Soldiers lined the sea front from South Parade Pier to Gilkicker Fort and Portsmouth's 20 dry docks and one floating dock were preparing further ships.

By 1910 the threat of German expansion was becoming apparent and strategy was now based on cooperation with the French. As a demonstration of

October/November 1914 saw the 2nd Oxfordshire and Buckinghamshire Light Infantry (predecessors of the Royal Green Jackets) repulse the Kaiser's Guard as their forebears did to Napoleon's Guard at Waterloo. But a sapping deadlock soon became established and before long 90,000 of the original 100,000 of the British Expeditionary Force were casualties.

In all, three million troops were stationed in or passed through Aldershot for their final six weeks training before crossing to France and the whole region provided men and garrison accommodation. But the Navy's demand for men and ships had a particular call on the area. In June 1916 the Battle of Jutland involving 148 British and 99 German ships was fought. Although the

2nd Battle Squadron at the Battle of Jutland, 31 May 1916. *Royal Naval Museum.*

FLEET AIR ARM MUSEUM, YEOVILTON. This museum houses over 50 historic aircraft telling the story of naval flying. There is also Concorde in its own exhibition hall.

Hampshire during the Great War.

1 Royal Aircraft Factory during World War 1.

2 ROYAL HAMPSHIRE REGIMENT MUSEUM
In the beautiful setting of Serle's House, Winchester, the collections of this famous regiment include decorations, medals, uniforms, weapons, paintings and photographs from all its campaigns.

outcome was considered indecisive, 6,000 men were lost, most from the Portsmouth area where virtually every family was affected.

Elsewhere the Hampshire Regiment and the Royal Marines found themselves involved in an attempt to defeat Germany's ally, Turkey, through the landings at Gallipoli. But the main war effort was in France where the newly developed tank, when used in mass formation, proved to have a decisive role in breaking the stalemate of trench warfare.

With the announcement of an armistice on 11 November 1918, many people thought that the 'Great War' would prove to be the war that ended all wars.

# THE INTERWAR YEARS

N 1919 THE Government laid down that all defence planning was to be based on the assumption that there would be no major war for 20 years and the role of the three services returned to that of the late Victorian era: policing the Empire. For the army at home it was generally a period of cutback with more going to the needs of the navy and RAF. In 1922, there were dramatic reductions with the disbandment of a number of Irish Regiments, and the amalgamation of many cavalry regiments.

When the wartime army had been demobilised, Aldershot outwardly returned to a peacetime routine though behind the scenes technological improvements were taking place, albeit slowly. Having shed aviation in 1912, the Royal Engineers now shed communications to the new Royal Corps of Signals for which Mons Barracks in Aldershot were built. Mechanisation of the cavalry began in 1928 when the 11th Hussars (Royal Hussars) exchanged their horses for armoured cars and the process accelerated throughout the 1930s. Conversion of the 1st Cavalry Brigade was completed in 1938 when they left Aldershot for Tidworth.

In recognition of its immense contribution to the country's war effort, the town of Aldershot was granted Borough status in 1922 (with three military councillors to be appointed by the Secretary of State) but to the general public at the time Aldershot meant only one thing, the Aldershot Command Tattoo which was the great annual military social event of the interwar years. From an attendance of 21,000 in 1921, it rose to over half a million in 1939.

During the interwar years there was the continual development of training and experimental units around work of R. J. Mitchell and the Supermarine Works at Woolston, and development on its advance design led to the Spitfire aircraft.

Calshot was the venue of the Schneider Trophy race in 1929 which was won by the RAF in a Supermarine S6 which broke the world air speed record five days later. A repeat victory and world record successes came in 1931 at Lee on the Solent. Calshot also had a part to play in the development of high speed launches for the RAF when a local businessman and the Portsmouth firm of Vospers worked on the development of air sea rescue launches

'Ancient Chivalry' from the 1933 Aldershot Command Tattoo.

Portsmouth harbour, whilst in the Dockyard itself most of the work was on repairs and refits rather than new construction.

In 1924 the Fleet Air Arm formed within the RAF which by then had already established a base in Gosport at Lee on the Solent. Since then the base has become an HM Seaplane Training School, an RN Air Station, an RAF Station and HQ of Coastal Command. Now, as HMS *Daedalus*, it is the Fleet Air Arm's training establishment.

The area's involvement in the development of aviation was one of the main features of this period. Calshot Castle again came to prominence in 1927 when the RAF High Speed Flight was based there for training on the Supermarine S5 seaplane which won the Schneider Trophy in Venice that year. The winning aircraft was the and Motor Torpedo Boats which were to prove valuable in future years.

The Isle of Wight was also involved as a pioneering area for aviation. Tommy Sopwith set up his first aircraft works there and the company J. S. White of Cowes diversified from their World War I destroyers into submarines and seaplanes.

By 1935, the fear of war was again in the air. The two reviews of the Fleet in 1935 and 1937 assembled an impressive array of naval craft. Dockyard work picked up in Portsmouth and in 1936 the first Spitfire flew at Eastleigh. The theme for the 1939 Aldershot Command Tattoo was national preparedness in the face of the looming Nazi threat. Few could have had much doubt by then that Europe was heading for conflict once again.

The Vickers Supermarine Prototype Spitfire at Eastleigh.

The Supermarine S6B Schneider Trophy Aircraft of 1931.

An advertisement for Supermarine soon after Sqn Ldr A. H. Orlebar established a new world speed record in 1929 flying the S6 N247.

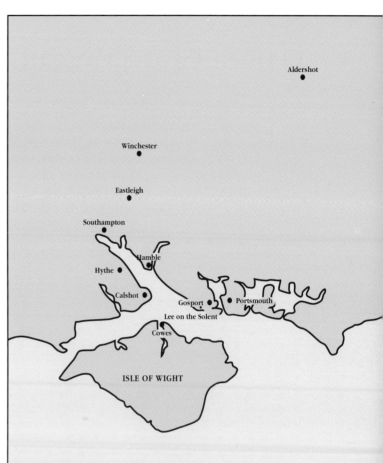

Hampshire during the Interwar Years.

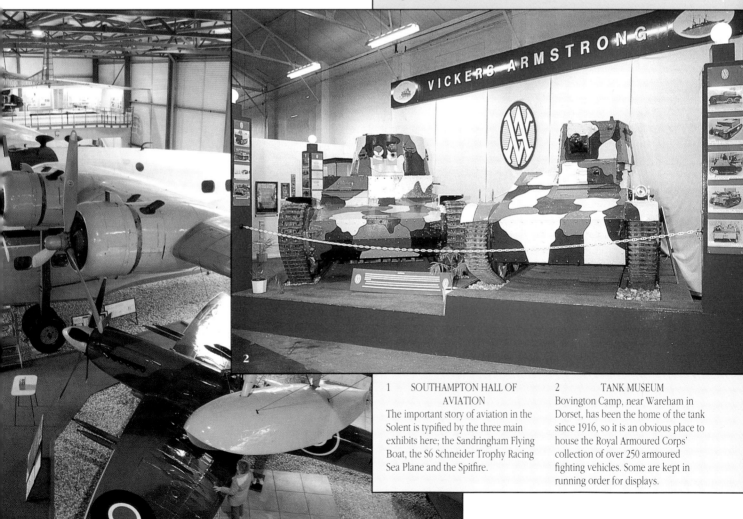

**1   SOUTHAMPTON HALL OF AVIATION**

The important story of aviation in the Solent is typified by the three main exhibits here; the Sandringham Flying Boat, the S6 Schneider Trophy Racing Sea Plane and the Spitfire.

**2   TANK MUSEUM**

Bovington Camp, near Wareham in Dorset, has been the home of the tank since 1916, so it is an obvious place to house the Royal Armoured Corps' collection of over 250 armoured fighting vehicles. Some are kept in running order for displays.

# THE SECOND WORLD WAR

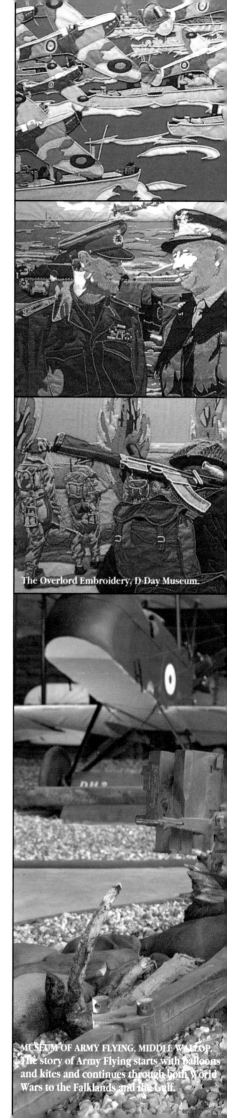

OR A REGION that had seen preparations for war many times over the centuries, there were to be striking similarities with the events that took place between 1939 and 1945. Expeditionary forces to France; Portsmouth and Southampton as the main embarkation ports; Portsmouth as the main base for the Royal Navy trying to keep open the nation's supply routes and seek out enemy battleships; fortifications adapted against renewed threat of invasion; and an increased pace of technological development.

Within three weeks of the outbreak of war, the camps and barracks around Aldershot were lying almost empty as 1st and 2nd Divisions led the British Expeditionary Force to France. As in 1914, thousands of Canadians volunteered for service and the 1st Canadian Division arrived, without equipment and largely untrained, at Christmas 1939 to fill the vacant barracks.

Hitler's invasion of Holland and Belgium brought the 'Phoney War' to a dramatic close. The British Expeditionary Force was split from the main French armies and driven back to effect its escape from the beaches of Dunkirk. Many small vessels set out from the Solent area to take part in Operation 'Dynamo' to rescue the troops. A surprising number of these craft are still around, including the *Folkestone Belle* which still serves on the Portsmouth Harbour Waterbus service.

Hitler launched the Luftwaffe to clear the skies of southern England before his invasion could take place. The Battle of Britain foiled these plans as the RAF managed to find sufficient Spitfires, Hurricanes and young pilots to fly from bases such as Tangmere, near Chichester. However, the attacks changed to air raids. In November 1940 two huge air raids destroyed the centre of Southampton.

River at Buckler's Hard produced naval motor launches and the Royal Marines were training Commandos at HMS *Cricket* now the site of Upper Hamble Country Park. The Hamble was also the secret home for X Craft submarines, assembled at Sarisbury Green before going on sea trials off Lee on the Solent. The planning and control of all these aspects of Operation 'Overlord' was done from Southwick House, north of Portsmouth.

Eventually all of central southern England became one enormous assembly point. It was finally on D-Day 6 June 1944, that an armada of 4,200 troop ships, and an escort of over 1,000 warships took this combined force of British, Canadian and American troops over to the beaches of Normandy. With the allied air forces flying over 14,000 sorties from airfields in Southern England and with the help of the Mulberry Harbours, a beach-head was soon secured which led to the liberation of Europe.

The Overlord Embroidery, D-Day Museum.

**HMS *Royal Oak* entering Portsmouth Harbour. *Royal Naval Museum***

The Portsmouth area received 67 air raids in total during which 930 civilians were killed and large parts of Portsmouth and Gosport destroyed.

Plans were already being made for a return to Europe. Soon the ports and creeks of Hampshire were busy assembling the vessels and equipment that would be required: vessels to carry 20,000 vehicles and over 150,000 men; specialist equipment such as the Mulberry Harbours; and the Pluto pipeline built at Woolston, Southampton and laid from the Isle of Wight to Cherbourg. A concrete section of a Mulberry Harbour can still be seen at Langstone harbour, and construction sites survive at Lepe Country Park, near Calshot, and on Hayling Island.

The River Hamble had seven slipways, the Beaulieu

The end of the war in Europe did not bring an end to military and naval activities. The Canadian Reinforcement Units in Aldershot became repatriation units and the camps were filled with thousands of soldiers expecting quick demobilisation. As the war continued in the Far East the available shipping was quite inadequate to meet the demands for reinforcements to India and the return home of hundreds of thousands of Canadians and Americans. Throughout the war the Canadian army had enjoyed particularly close and good relations with Aldershot and the surrounding towns and villages. This was recognised by the granting of the Freedom of the Borough to the Canadian Army Overseas in September 1945, the only occasion on which a whole army has been awarded such an honour.

MUSEUM OF ARMY FLYING, MIDDLE WALLOP. The story of Army Flying starts with balloons and kites and continues through both World Wars to the Falklands and the Gulf.

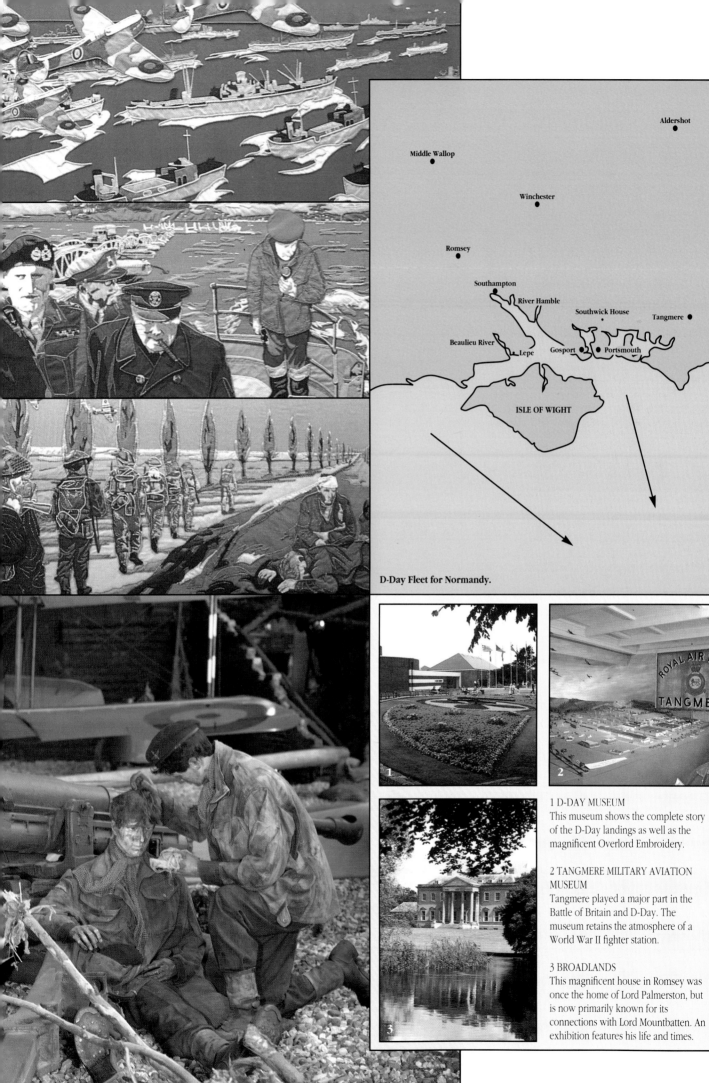

**D-Day Fleet for Normandy.**

Aldershot

Middle Wallop

Winchester

Romsey

Southampton

River Hamble

Southwick House

Tangmere

Beaulieu River

Lepe

Gosport

Portsmouth

ISLE OF WIGHT

ROYAL AIR FORCE TANGMERE

**1 D-DAY MUSEUM**
This museum shows the complete story of the D-Day landings as well as the magnificent Overlord Embroidery.

**2 TANGMERE MILITARY AVIATION MUSEUM**
Tangmere played a major part in the Battle of Britain and D-Day. The museum retains the atmosphere of a World War II fighter station.

**3 BROADLANDS**
This magnificent house in Romsey was once the home of Lord Palmerston, but is now primarily known for its connections with Lord Mountbatten. An exhibition features his life and times.

# THE NUCLEAR AGE

THE SECOND WORLD WAR was brought to an abrupt end in August 1945 when atomic bombs were dropped on Hiroshima and Nagasaki heralding the Nuclear Age. While hundreds of thousands of wartime servicemen came back home to be demobilised, 1st and 2nd Divisions never returned to Aldershot, staying in Germany first as an army of occupation and then as Britain's contribution to NATO.

Already the home of the well known Mons Officer Cadet School, where by 1962 40,000 wartime and National Service officers had been commissioned, Aldershot became a great training centre for the Army and the home of the Parachute Regiment, famous for its actions in Normandy, at Arnhem and on the Rhine.

While the growing armouries of nuclear weapons maintained a tense peace in Europe, numerous conventional wars and lesser local conflicts were fought by the British forces elsewhere in the world from Palestine through Korea, Malaya, Borneo, Cyprus to the Falklands and the Gulf. Nonetheless, as Britain withdrew from Empire its armed forces were gradually reduced in size and in 1962 the last National Servicemen were released. Fixed shore batteries became obsolete, 'Coastal defence' was abolished in 1956 and over the succeeding years fortifications along the South Coast, such as Southsea Castle and the Palmerston Forts, found new roles as places of historic interest, museums and activity centres.

With the end of National Service many regiments were amalgamated and new ones formed. Among those amalgamations were The Light Infantry formed from five county light infantry regiments, the sixth joining the Kings Royal Rifle Corps and the Rifle Brigade to form the Royal Green Jackets, both new regiments being based in Winchester. In Aldershot the old Victorian Barracks were pulled down and new depots and training centres were built for the transport, medical, ordnance, dental, PT, catering and nursing corps, all having their regimental museums there.

The Royal Navy experienced its full share of cuts too. The last Portsmouth-built warship, the frigate *Andromeda*, was completed in 1968. The Royal Dockyard showed what it could do in an emergency when the Task Force was sent to recover the Falkland Islands. The Task Force's aircraft carriers, *Hermes* and *Invincible*, sailed from Portsmouth for the South Atlantic on 5 April 1982. After a successful campaign, in which Royal Marine Commandos and the Parachute Regiment played a distinguished role, the Falklands were retaken, and the ships and men of the Task Force returned to a hero's welcome at Portsmouth.

1    LIGHT INFANTRY MUSEUM
This museum in Winchester depicts the achievements of the Light Infantry from its formation in 1968 to the present day. Exhibits include part of the Berlin Wall and the Gulf War of 1991.

2    The Task Force returns from the Falklands. HMS *Hermes* in 1982. © *Crown Copyright 1992 MoD*

3    AIRBORNE FORCES MUSEUM
the history of those who fought as part of the Airborne Forces from 1940 to the present day is portrayed in this museum in Aldershot. Original briefing models are included among the exhibits.

4    ROYAL SIGNALS MUSEUM
This museum in Blandford covers the history of army communications from the Crimean War to the Gulf War and includes a collection of Second World War spy radios.